Table of Contents

Get a Move On!

Books
of the Bible
Games

by Rhoda Preston
and LeeDell Stickler

Abingdon Press

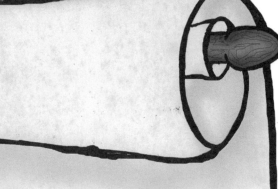

Abingdon's
Books of the Bible Games

ISBN 0-687-49480-X

Writers: Rhoda Preston and LeeDell Stickler

Editor: LeeDell Stickler

Production Editor: Cindy Harris

Production and Design Manager: R.E. Osborne

Designer: Paige Easter

Cover Design: R.E. Osborne

06 07 08 09 10 11 12 13 14—10 9 8 7 6 5 4 3 2

Manufactured in the United States of America

Reproducibles

To the Teacher

What Is This Book All About?

Genesis, Exodus, Leviticus, and uh, what comes next? Who among us has not come across a Bible verse and had to sort through our memory trying to remember just where in the Bible the book is located? First we had to decide if it was in the Old Testament or the New Testament. Then we had to think about the order of the books. Once upon a time, most of us learned the books of the Bible in order using whatever memory tricks we had up our sleeve. Then when we weren't under pressure or fear of letting our Bible skills team down, we promptly forgot them again. But help is on the way!

Books of the Bible Games uses a variety of games to teach what used to be a laborious chore for children—learning the books of the Bible in order, by category and by section. These games are simple and can be done with little pre-class preparation once the sets of game cards are completed. Some of the games incorporate movement, which adds another dimension to the skill.

Why Use Games?

Games have many benefits and encourage many positive life skills:

- Games focus and channel energy.

- Games help children develop socially, emotionally, intellectually, and physically.

- Games develop skills of concentration, memory, creativity, problem solving, and decision making.

- Games build bonds of communication and friendship.

- Games build independence, self-esteem, and confidence.

- Games teach children to handle healthy competition.

- Games encourage children to strive to do their best and appreciate their capabilities as well as their limitations.

- Games encourage children to appreciate the capabilities and limitations of others.

- Finally, and perhaps most importantly, games are fun!

Studies suggest that active children experience less stress. Games nurture the whole child—body, intellect, emotion, and spirit—allowing learning and child development to take place in a spontaneous and natural manner.

How Do I Use This Book?

Getting started is much simpler than you think.

- Beginning with children whose reading skills are limited is counterproductive. Children who are struggling with three-letter and four-letter words are hardly ready to tackle words such as *Obadiah*, *Habakkuk*, *Zechariah*, and *Thessalonians*. (These are hard enough for adults.) Don't set yourself up for failure (or worse still, make the children feel like failures) by asking too much too soon.

- Make a set of Books of the Bible Cards (pages 56–64) for each child in the class, plus an extra set for the teacher and/or the classroom. If possible, photocopy each set onto cardstock. Cut the cards apart and store in a plastic resealable bag.

- Plan the learning experience to be as noncompetitive as possible. Now, as my son once said, "What fun is a game if there isn't any winner?" A little competition is not harmful, but that doesn't mean you have to turn each learning experience into a war between factions. Games should be fun. Through games children learn about teamwork, fair play, and personal success. Not every activity can be arranged as a noncompetitive game. Children will never go through life *not* having to compete. But try to provide a variety of game experiences, some competitive, some cooperative.

- Make the games an integral part of the Sunday-morning lesson. Set aside a special time when these Bible skills are honed and polished. Substitute a Books of the Bible game for another activity in the lesson plan. Plan a Wednesday-night game night where you focus on these Bible skills alone. You will find the children looking forward to showing off their skills.

Adapting for Different Age or Skill Levels

We want the Bible to be accessible to our children. We know that inside the pages of the Bible are stories, verses, and other things that will impact their lives. But first they have to be able to use it. We are also aware that there is a great deal of difference between the skills of a second or third grader and a fifth or sixth grader. Each game will have suggestions on how to adapt the game for skilled and less skilled players. (Sometimes this has nothing to do with age.)

Now, Have Fun!

Mostly Just the Cards

Easy Does It!

For This Section You Will Need:

- a set of Books of the Bible Cards (pages 56–64) for each child in the class

- a set of Books of the Bible Cards for the teacher and/or the class

- a resealable plastic bag for each set of cards

Note: Copy the Old Testament cards on one color of cardstock and the New Testament cards on another color. This makes it easier to distinguish between the two when separating the cards.

Begin small, with just a few cards. You didn't learn to read by picking up the encyclopedia. But a teacher I once knew said that you can eat a car if you break it into small enough pieces. With younger, less skilled children, begin with four or five books. With older, more advanced children, you can begin with ten or more.

Start with the books of the Old Testament and, when they have been mastered, go on to the New Testament, or vice versa. Provide a flat working space so that the children can spread out their cards. If table space is an issue, use the floor instead.

Starting Simple

Instructions

You will need:
    Books of the Bible Cards (pages 56–64)
    Bag or basket

Begin your quest to have the children learn the names and the order of the books of the Bible with this simple game. You will need only two sets of cards—one for the teacher and one for the class.

Step 1: Distribute the cards equally among the children. (The number will vary depending on how skilled the children are at recognizing the books of the Bible.)

Step 2: Identify each of the books you will be using, holding up the card, saying the name, and letting the children repeat the name after you. Use a pronunciation guide if you feel uncomfortable on your own.

Step 3: Place the second set of cards in a bag or a basket.

Step 4: Draw a card from the bag and read it aloud.

Step 5: Whichever child in the group is holding that card stands up and says the name of the book of the Bible.

Adapting the game: For more skilled children, use the entire set of cards, giving each child an equal number of cards. To limit the number of books, stick to either the Old Testament or the New Testament.

Order, Please!

Instructions

You will need:
- Books of the Bible Cards (pages 56–64)
    - Old Testament—sequential books
    - New Testament—sequential books
- Books of the Bible Bookshelves (pages 50–51)
- Resealable plastic bags
- Bibles

Step 1: Place the first five Books of the Bible Cards from the Old Testament (Genesis through Deuteronomy) or the New Testament (Matthew through Acts) in resealable plastic bags, one set for each child. (Reserve the remaining cards for future weeks.)

Step 2: Identify each of the five books, holding up the card, saying the name, and letting the children repeat the name after you. Use a pronunciation guide if you feel uncomfortable on your own.

Step 3: Each child mixes up the five cards.

Step 4: Each child places the cards back in the correct order. If the children need assistance, they can use the Books of the Bible Bookshelves.

Step 5: Help the children practice finding the five books in a Bible.

Step 6: The children place each set back into its resealable bag for next time.

Play this game as many times as it takes for the children to become familiar with the first five books of the Old Testament and the New Testament.

Adapting for more skilled children: Once the children have mastered the first groups of books, add five more. Continue until the children can do an entire Testament at one time.

Switch Engine

Instructions

You will need:
 Books of the Bible Cards (pages 56–64)
  Old Testament—sequential books
  New Testament—sequential books
 Resealable plastic bags

Begin this game with five cards in a sequence. For example, Genesis through Deuteronomy, or Matthew through Acts.

Step 1: Place the five sequential Books of the Bible Cards in resealable plastic bags, one set for each child. (Reserve the remaining cards for future weeks.)

Step 2: Distribute the sets of cards, one set per child.

Step 3: Identify each of the books, holding up the card, saying the name, and letting the children repeat the name after you.

Step 4: Divide the class into pairs.

Step 5: Explain to the children that the line of cards is a "train." Each book of the Bible is a "train car." The purpose of the game is to get the train cars in order. The first card in the sequence will be the engine. (If using Genesis through Deuteronomy, Genesis will be the engine. If using Matthew through Acts, Matthew will be the engine.) The last card will be the caboose.

Step 6: Each child shuffles his or her cards and places them in a line.

Step 7: The players in each pair take turns. At each turn, the player can switch two of his or her cards around. The first player in each pair to get his or her cards in order wins.

Adapting for more skilled children: As the children become more skilled at ordering the books of the Bible, you can increase the number of cards. Do it gradually so that the children don't feel overwhelmed.

1, 2, 3, Go!

Instructions

You will need:
Books of the Bible Cards (pages 56–64)
   Old Testament—sequential books
   New Testament—sequential books
Bibles
Resealable plastic bags

Begin this game with five cards in a sequence, for example, Genesis through Deuteronomy, or Matthew through Acts. If you are using these games progressively, after the children have mastered the first five books, increase the number to ten. Make sure the children have mastered them before moving forward.

Step 1: Divide the class into groups of three.

Step 2: Place the sequential Books of the Bible Cards in resealable plastic bags, one set for each group. (Reserve the remaining cards for future weeks.)

Step 3: Distribute the sets of cards, one set per group.

Step 4: Identify each of the books, holding up the card, saying the name, and letting the children repeat the name after you.

Step 5: The children work together in their groups to put the cards in order on the table.

Step 6: When each group's cards are in order, give each child a Bible.

Step 7: Call out one of the books on the cards. Then say "1, 2, 3, Go!" The first person in each group to find that book in the Bible takes that card from the table. Continue calling out books until all cards have been taken. The person in each group with the most cards wins.

Adapting for more skilled children: Increase the number of books in the sequence.

Concentrate

Instructions

You will need:
Books of the Bible Cards (pages 56–64)
Resealable plastic bags

Step 1: Place a chosen number of Books of the Bible Cards in resealable plastic bags, one set for each child. (Reserve the remaining cards for future weeks.)

Step 2: Distribute the sets of cards, one set per child.

Step 3: Identify each of the books in the bag, holding up the card, saying the name, and letting the children repeat the name after you.

Step 4: Divide the class into pairs.

Step 5: Each pair mixes their sets of Bible cards together and lays the cards facedown on the table in random order.

Step 6: Each player takes a turn turning up two cards, looking for a match. If the two cards match, the player says the name of the book out loud, keeps the matching cards, and takes an extra turn. If the cards don't match, the player turns them back over, and play passes to the second player. When all cards have been matched, the player with the most cards wins.

Step 7: At the conclusion of the game, ask each pair to separate their cards into two sets again and place each set in its plastic bag.

Adapting for more skilled children: Begin with six or seven cards from each child's bag. Make sure they are the same cards. Then add more cards as the children become more skilled at knowing these books.

What Comes Next?

Instructions

You will need:
Books of the Bible Cards (pages 56–64)
    Old Testament—sequential books
    New Testament—sequential books
Resealable plastic bags

Step 1: Distribute plastic bags with a chosen number of Books of the Bible Cards inside, one set per child.

Step 2: Identify each of the books, holding up the card, saying the name, and letting the children repeat the name after you.

Step 3: Each child mixes up his or her individual cards and spreads them faceup on the table.

Step 4: Call out the name of a book of the Bible.

Step 5: The children look at their cards and find the book that comes next. For example, if you call out Exodus, the children find Leviticus. If you call out John, the children find Acts.

Adapting for more skilled children: Begin this game with no more than ten cards in a sequence. Add books in increments of five. Make sure the children have mastered the ten before moving forward.

Who's Up First?

Instructions

You will need:
Books of the Bible Cards (pages 56–64)
   Old Testament—sequential books
   New Testament—sequential books
Books of the Bible Bookshelves (pages 50–51)
Resealable plastic bags

Step 1: Choose an even number of sequential cards to use. The number should depend on the children's skill level. Identify each book of the Bible that you will be using, holding up the card, saying the name, and letting the children repeat the name after you.

Step 2: Divide the class into pairs. Distribute plastic bags with the chosen Books of the Bible Cards inside, one bag per pair.

Step 3: Each pair shuffles the cards and deals them out between the two children. Each player places his or her cards face-down in a stack.

Step 4: Both players turn over their top card at the same time.

Step 5: The person whose book comes first in the Bible takes both cards. If the children can't remember which book comes first, let them check their Books of the Bible Bookshelves.

Step 6: Continue playing until all cards have been turned over. The player with the most cards wins. At the conclusion of the game, place each set of cards in its plastic resealable bag.

Adapting for more skilled children: Have the children add more cards and use the table of contents of their individual Bibles to confirm or deny the correctness of an answer.

Stopwatch!

Instructions

You will need:
- Books of the Bible Cards (pages 56–64)
  - Old Testament—sequential books
  - New Testament—sequential books
- Books of the Bible Bookshelves (pages 50–51)
- Bibles
- Resealable plastic bags

Step 1: Identify each book of the Bible that you will be using, holding up the card, saying the name, and letting the children repeat the name after you.

Step 2: Divide the class into groups of three. Distribute plastic bags with the chosen Books of the Bible Cards inside, one bag per group.

Step 3: Each group shuffles one set of cards and spreads them out faceup on the table.

Step 4: At the signal, the children see how quickly their team can put all the cards in the correct order. If they need help, they may use the Books of the Bible Bookshelves or the table of contents of their Bibles to check their answer. Use a stopwatch to time the teams.

Step 5: As each group completes the ordering, write down how much time it took.

Step 6: After everyone has the books in order, repeat the names of the books in unison.

Step 7: Play the game again, with each group trying to beat their previous times.

Step 8: At the conclusion of the game, place each set of cards in its own plastic bag.

Adapting the game: The number of cards you use will determine whether the game is appropriate for skilled or less skilled children. Start with a small number, such as five or six, and move progressively higher.

Sandwich

Instructions

You will need:
- Books of the Bible Cards (pages 56–64)
  - Old Testament—sequential books
  - New Testament—sequential books
- Resealable plastic bags

With younger children, begin with no more than ten cards.

Step 1: Identify each book of the Bible that you will be using, holding up the card, saying the name, and letting the children repeat the name after you.

Step 2: Divide the class into pairs. Distribute plastic bags with the chosen Books of the Bible Cards inside, one bag per pair.

Step 3: Each pair shuffles one set of cards and spreads them faceup on the table. Keep a set for the "caller" (teacher or another child).

Step 4: In this game the books of the Bible are parts of a sandwich. Call out a book of the Bible. That book is the "filling" of the sandwich.

Step 5: The children find that card then find the "bread" for the sandwich—the books that come right before and right after the book that was called. They put all three cards together, making a sandwich. For example, if the caller calls out the book of Exodus, the pair of children find Genesis, Exodus, and Leviticus.

Adapting for more skilled children: Use all the New Testament cards or all the Old Testament cards.

Books of the Bible Bingo

Instructions

You will need:
Books of the Bible Cards (pages 56–64)
Basket or bag

This is a good name recognition game that doesn't require a great amount of skill. Most children can participate even if their identification skills are somewhat limited. Use all the cards for a group of older children, or limit the cards to either the Old Testament or New Testament for younger children.

Step 1: Give each child a bag with the chosen number of Books of the Bible Cards inside.

Step 2: The children shuffle the cards.

Step 3: The children deal twenty-five cards faceup onto the table and arrange the cards in a five-card by five-card square. Each card will act as a space on their Bingo card.

Step 4: Keep one set of cards for the "caller." Place these cards in a basket or bag.

Step 5: The caller draws a Book of the Bible Card from the basket or bag and reads the name aloud.

Step 6: Children who have that book of the Bible on their Bingo card (their set of cards) will either place a piece of paper on that book or turn the card over.

Step 7: The first player to get five in a row wins the game.

Adapting for less skilled children: Instead of using twenty-five cards, limit the number of cards to sixteen. The children will create a four-card by four-card square. Proceed with the game from there.

Flashlight

Instructions

You will need:
Books of the Bible Cards (pages 56–64)
Flashlight for each pair of children

Step 1: Divide the class into pairs.

Step 2: Distribute one set of Books of the Bible Cards to each pair.

Step 3: Each pair shuffles the set of cards and deals the cards equally between them, with one card left over. They place the leftover card faceup on the table between them.

Step 4: Each child places his or her cards facedown in a stack on the table.

Step 5: Shut off the lights, and give each team a flashlight. Both players turn over their top card at the same time.

Step 6: While the second player holds the flashlight, the first player arranges the three turned up cards (the two that the players turned over and the leftover card) in biblical order.

Step 7: Now it is the second player's turn. Both players turn over their top card at the same time. While the first player holds the flashlight, the second player adds those two cards to the cards on the table, arranging all five in biblical order.

Step 8: Play continues until all cards have been placed in a long line on the table. The first pair to get their books completely in order wins.

Adapting the game: If the children already have a working knowledge of all the books of the Bible in order, then use all the cards. If the children are still "working on it," then use a smaller number. Make sure the number of cards is an odd number, for example 19, 25, 29, and so forth.

Find It!

Instructions

You will need:
    Books of the Bible Cards (pages 56–64)
    Bibles
    Index cards
    Marker

Just learning the names of the books of the Bible is a start, but there is a more practical side. As the children become more familiar with the names and the order of the books of the Bible, they are able to look up verses more easily. This game gives some practical experience in using the Bible.

Step 1: Give each child a Bible and a set of the Books of the Bible Cards.

Step 2: Choose Bible references from the group of books you are working with today, one reference for each book. Write each reference on an index card.

Step 3: The children find the Books of the Bible Cards for the various books from which the references have been chosen.

Step 4: The children arrange the book cards in sequential order.

Step 5: The children look up the verses in their individual Bibles.

Step 6: Invite the children to read the verses aloud.

Short Books Search

Instructions

You will need:
Books of the Bible Cards (pages 56–64)
Bibles
Posterboard, marker

Some of the books of the Bible are extremely short (6 chapters or fewer) compared to the others. These can be found in both the Old Testament and the New Testament. To begin this exercise, choose only New Testament books or Old Testament books.

Old Testament short books: Ruth, Lamentations, Joel, Obadiah, Jonah, Nahum, Habakkuk, Zephaniah, Haggai, Malachi

New Testament short books: Galatians, Ephesians, Philippians, Colossians, 1 Thessalonians, 2 Thessalonians, 1 Timothy, 2 Timothy, Titus, Philemon, James, 1 Peter, 2 Peter, 1 John, 2 John, 3 John, Jude

Step 1: Write the names of the "short" books you have chosen to use for this activity. Read the name of each of the books, and have the children say the name after you.

Step 2: Distribute the plastic bags with the Books of the Bible Cards inside. The children locate the cards of the book names you read and place them in sequential order.

Step 3: The children find each book in their Bibles and note the number of chapters each one has.

Answers:

Old Testament Books— Ruth (4), Lamentations (5), Joel (3), Obadiah (1), Jonah (4), Nahum (3), Habakkuk (3), Zephaniah (3), Haggai (2), and Malachi (4).

New Testament Books— Galatians (6), Ephesians (6), Philippians (4), Colossians (4), 1 Thessalonians (5), 2 Thessalonians (3), 1 Timothy (6), 2 Timothy (4), Titus (3), Philemon (1), James (5), 1 Peter (5), 2 Peter (3), 1 John (5), 2 John (1), 3 John (1), Jude (1).

Old Testament or New?

Instructions

You will need:
Bible Books Category Markers (page 54)
Books of the Bible Cards (pages 56–64)
Books of the Bible Bookshelves (pages 50–51)

Once the children have mastered the names of the books of the Bible and can put them in the correct order, the next most important step is to learn the various categories that these books fit into. The Bible is more than just one book. It is a library of books that come together to tell the story of God's interaction with the world in past history and today.

Step 1: Make a copy of the Bible Books Category Markers for each team.

Step 2: Divide the class into teams of three or four children.

Step 3: Give each team a set of Books of the Bible Cards and a set of Bible Books Category Markers. Each team spreads the category markers faceup on the table.

Step 4: Each team shuffles the cards and places them facedown in a stack on the table.

Step 5: Each team turns up the top card in the stack and tries to place the card in its appropriate category.

Step 6: Let the children use the Books of the Bible Bookshelves to check their stacks.

Adapting the game: For younger children use only New Testament cards or Old Testament cards. For older children use both sets combined.

Category Match

Instructions

You will need:
  Books of the Bible Cards (pages 56–64)
  Books of the Bible Bookshelves (pages 50–51)

Helping the children come to know the related books of the Bible is a hard task. Turn it into a card game and watch how easy it becomes. The game is similar to Crazy Eights or Old Maid. The children will look at the cards in their hands and decide to collect either Law cards, History cards, Poetry/Wisdom cards, Prophecy/Prophets cards, Gospels cards, or Letters cards.

Step 1: Divide the class into groups of four.

Step 2: Give each group a set of the Books of the Bible Cards.

Step 3: Each group shuffles the cards, deals eight cards to each child at the table, stacks the remaining cards in the center of the table, and turns over the top card from the stack, placing it faceup on the table.

Step 4: The players take turns either taking the faceup card or drawing a card from the deck. After each player takes a card, the player must then discard one card from his or her hand.

Step 5: When a child has a "book," or four cards from the same category, he or she lays them faceup on the table.

Step 6: The child who collects the most "books" wins.

Books of the Bible Scavenger Hunt

Instructions

You will need:

Scavenger Hunt Questions—Level 1 or Level 2 (pages 52–53)
Books of the Bible Cards (pages 56–64)
Bible for each team
Pencils

This game is particularly fun on a retreat weekend when the children get their Bibles. Not only does it give the children a familiarity with the books of the Bible, but it also gives them practice in using the Bible.

There are two levels of questions: one set for the beginner Bible users and one set for children who are fairly skilled in Bible usage.

Step 1: Divide the class into teams of two or three. Pair children who are less skilled with children who are more skilled.

Step 2: Give each team a set of Scavenger Hunt Questions, a set of Books of the Bible Cards, and a Bible.

Step 3: Set a time limit for finding the answers to all the Scavenger Hunt Questions. If you have a younger group playing the game, set a longer playing time.

Step 4: The teams earn a point for each question they are able to answer. The winning team is the one with the most points.

Good Guess

Instructions

You will need:
Books of the Bible Cards (pages 56–64)
Chalkboard, chalk
Individually wrapped candies, or colored plastic drinking straws

This game is played with teams. A team can have as few as one member or as many as ten. If you want to cut the calories, substitute colored plastic drinking straws for the individually wrapped candies.

Step 1: Divide the class into two teams. Each team selects a captain.

Step 2: Mix up the Books of the Bible Cards.

Step 3: Invite one of the team captains to come forward and draw a card.

Step 4: The captain draws a blank line on the chalkboard for each of the letters in the name of the book of the Bible. Place ten pieces of candy (or ten drinking straws) on the table.

Step 5: The teams take turns guessing letters that might be in the word. For every correct letter, the captain writes the letter on the appropriate line. For every incorrect letter, the teacher removes a piece of candy (or drinking straw).

Step 6: During each team's turn, that team can stop the play and make a guess as to what word is on the board. If the guess is correct, the team collects however many candies are left. If the guess is incorrect, the other team gets the candies.

Step 7: Repeat steps 3 through 6. Continue playing until the children are tired of the game.

Adapting for less skilled children: For younger children, you might want to use only the shorter book names and start with only five pieces of candy. At the end of the game, if you are using candy, designate the winner, but make sure each team has an equal share of the rewards.

Slap Syllables

Instructions

You will need:
Books of the Bible Cards (pages 56–64)
Five squares of colored paper for each child
Markers or crayons

This is a good game to aid with the pronunciation of the different books of the Bible. Breaking words into syllables is one of the best tools for this. Any number of children can play.

Step 1: Give each child five squares of colored paper. The children write the numbers 1 through 5, one on each square. The children place the squares on the table in front of them in order.

Step 2: Shuffle the Books of the Bible Cards. Draw out one of the cards and read the name aloud.

Step 3: The children "slap" their hand down on the number that indicates how many syllables are in the name of the book. For example, *Ezekiel* has four syllables. Numbers do not count as syllables.

Step 4: Pronounce the name one more time, slowly, so that the children can easily count the number to check themselves.

Get a Move On!

Movement Is Good!

For This Section You Will Need:

- a set of Books of the Bible Cards (pages 56–64) for each child in the class

- a set of Books of the Bible Cards for the teacher and/or the class

- a resealable plastic bag for each set of cards

Helps for the Teacher: Children learn through movement. For many of your children, physical movement is a preferred learning style. Including movement with a Bible skill doubles the likelihood that the children will learn. Don't be afraid to get a little "rowdy," but there are some "rules of the road."

1. For games that require movement, you will need to plan ahead. Practice the game yourself to make sure you understand exactly how it should be played.

2. Put safety first. Clear the area of any hazards. Check for slippery floors and remove any rugs or objects that might trip a child who is in motion.

3. Be aware of disabilities. If a child in your classroom has a physical disability, use games that will let that child participate on an equal level with the others. Avoid games that put the child at a disadvantage.

4. Create balance in your teaching. You would not want to play an active game just prior to a time when you want the children to sit quietly. Use movement games as a "brain break" from more sedentary activities.

5. Play cooperatively. Whenever possible, remove the element of competition from the game you play. However, since children do love to compete, provide opportunities for some competition. Having fun should be more important than winning.

Places, Please

Instructions

You will need:
- Books of the Bible Cards (pages 56–64)
- Basket or bag
- Kitchen timer
- Bibles, or Books of the Bible Bookshelves (pages 50–51)

When the children have become familiar with the books of the Bible, this is a good game to try. It will work with a larger group or a smaller group. Choose Books of the Bible Cards from a particular group, such as the Law or Gospels (easy), or the Prophets or Letters (harder).

Step 1: Place the cards you plan to use in a basket or bag.

Step 2: One by one, every child reaches in the bag and draws out a card, holds up the card, and pronounces the name of the book of the Bible that he or she is holding.

Step 3: Set the timer for the allotted amount of time (two to three minutes for a small group of cards, longer for a larger group).

Step 4: Say "go." The children then arrange themselves in the order of the books in the Bible. Use the table of contents in a Bible or the Books of the Bible Bookshelves chart to check their arrangement.

Cool Options:

Option 1—If you have a larger class and can divide the class into teams, create a little healthy competition.

Option 2—If you want to avoid competition altogether, simply time the children until they are in the correct order. Then let them put their cards back in the bag or basket, draw them out, and try again. The object is to do it faster each time.

Who Am I?

Instructions

You will need:
Books of the Bible Cards (pages 56–64)
Masking tape

This game is best played when the children are reasonably comfortable with the names and the arrangement of the books of the Bible.

Step 1: As the children come into the room, tape one of the Books of the Bible Cards on each child's back and give each child a set of Books of the Bible Cards.

Step 2: The children ask one another questions about their book that can be answered with either a yes or a no in order to discover which book they have on their back, for example, Am I in the Old Testament? Am I one of the Gospels? Am I a short name?

Step 3: The last child to discover who he or she is has to pay a silly and non-threatening penalty, such as singing "Mary Had a Little Lamb" while standing on one foot.

Adapting for less skilled children: Let the children know ahead of time which books you will be using. For example, use only Paul's letters, or only the Gospels. (You can have duplicate cards for the shorter, more familiar books of the Bible, such as those in the Law or History.)

Cool Option: When a child discovers what book of the Bible is on his or her back, he or she gets a Bible and locates that book.

Balloon Bop

Instructions

You will need:
    Books of the Bible Cards (pages 56–64)
    Balloons (one for each child)
    Tape
    CD, CD player
    Bibles, or Books of the Bible Bookshelves (pages 50–51)

This game requires a bit more space and involves more movement. Since balloons have a tendency to go in many directions, make sure the area is clear of any hazards that can create a problem. Choose a category of books of the Bible unless your children are ready to tackle random books.

Step 1: Give each child a deflated balloon.

Step 2: The children blow up their balloons and tie them off, then tape a Book of the Bible Card to each balloon.

Step 3: Begin the music. The children bat the balloons around in the area as the music plays.

Step 4: When the music stops, the children grab the nearest balloon and race to put themselves in order.

Step 5: Check the accuracy of the order by using the table of contents in the Bible or the Books of the Bible Bookshelves chart in the back of this book.

Adapting for more skilled children: If you have children who are very comfortable with the books of the Bible, mix it up with a random selection. For example, Genesis, 1 Samuel, Ezekiel, Malachi, Luke, and Revelation. This would create quite a challenge. You can also use only Old Testament books or only New Testament books.

Really Rowdy Relay

Instructions

You will need:
  Books of the Bible Cards (pages 56–64)
  Masking tape
  Balloons
  Bibles, or Books of the Bible Bookshelves (pages 50–51)

This activity will help the children work off a little excess energy and become more familiar with the books of the Bible and their order.

Step 1: Divide the class into pairs. Place a masking tape starting line and finish line about twenty feet apart in an open space.

Step 2: Give each team a set of Books of the Bible Cards and a balloon for each card.

Step 3: The children blow up the balloons and tie them off, then tape one of the Books of the Bible Cards onto each balloon.

Step 4: Player A in each team goes to the starting line. Player B waits at the finish line.

Step 5: When the teacher says "go," Player A selects a balloon from the pile for his or her team, places it between his or her knees, and jumps along, feet together, toward the finish line. At the finish line, Player A sets the balloon on the ground.

Step 6: Player B runs back to the starting line, gets a balloon, and repeats the process. When Player B gets to the finish line, he or she places the two balloons in the correct order.

Step 7: Player A returns to the starting line for another balloon. Play continues until all the balloons are at the finish line and are in the correct order. Check the accuracy of the order against the table of contents in a Bible or the Books of the Bible Bookshelves chart.

Library Search

Instructions

You will need:
Books of the Bible Bookshelves (pages 50–51)
Books of the Bible Cards (pages 56–64)
Wooden dowels with a red paper flag attached to each
Small paper cups with clay on the bottom

Step 1: Make a copy of the Books of the Bible Bookshelves for each team. Divide the class into teams of three or four. Give each team a cup. Each team selects a "reporter" for each round of the game.

Step 2: Deal out one set of Books of the Bible Cards equally among the teams. The teams place the cards facedown on the table.

Step 3: At the signal, the teams turn up the first card in their pile.

Step 4: Give the teams a time limit to find the book on the Books of the Bible Bookshelves. When a team believes they have accomplished this, the reporter raises his or her hand. An adult spotter checks the response and, if the answer is correct, places a flag in the team's cup.

Step 5: The teams earn one point for each book that they locate on the Bookshelves. Play continues until all cards have been turned over. At the end of the first round, tally the number of points for the teams.

Adapting for less skilled children:

Option 1—Limit the books of the Bible to either the Old Testament or the New Testament for a simpler game.

Option 2—Extend the amount of time allowed for each of the location stages in the game.

Cool Option: After the teams locate their books on the Bookshelves, have them locate the books in a Bible. Give them a time limit. Each team has an assigned "looker." At the signal, the looker finds the book of the Bible and then raises a hand for the adult spotter. When the book has been verified, the team earns a second point.

Book Search

Instructions

You will need:
Books of the Bible Cards (pages 56–64), one set for the class
Two similar (or identical) obstacle courses

This game not only reinforces the order of the books of the Bible, it also creates a sense of teamwork. Be conscious of the physical abilities of the children in your class. For example, if crawling under a chair might be difficult, use a table instead.

Step 1: Shuffle the Books of the Bible Cards.

Step 2: Divide the class into two teams.

Step 3: Give each team four to six cards. Place the remaining cards on a table at the end of the obstacle course.

Step 4: Give the teams three minutes to arrange the cards that they have in the order in which they are found in the Bible.

Step 5: When both teams have their cards in order, the teacher says "go." The first member of the team crawls through the obstacle course to the table where the remaining Books of the Bible Cards are, selects one card, and crawls back through the obstacle course to the remaining team members.

Step 6: While the remaining team members are placing that card in order with the others that the team has previously ordered, the second player crawls through the obstacle course and retrieves another card.

Step 7: Continue until all the cards have been placed.

Step 8: The winner is the team with the most cards in the correct order.

Cool Option: Assign each team a different category of books (or two if a category is particularly short, for example, Law and Gospels). (See pages 50–51). The first player goes through the obstacle course, finds a book in the assigned category, and brings it back. Subsequent players do the same.

Hip-Hop Bible Books

Instructions

You will need:
- Books of the Bible Cards (pages 56–64)
- Masking tape
- Bean bags, smooth stones, or other tokens for markers

For a large class, set up more than one playing grid so that it will move faster.

Step 1: Lay out a typical hopscotch playing grid. Number the squares as shown.

Step 2: Shuffle the Books of the Bible Cards. Place one card in each square. Secure the cards with masking tape.

Step 3: The two basic rules of hopscotch are that you can only have one foot in each square, and that you have to hop over the square with the marker in it.

Step 4: The first player tosses the marker into the first square. That player hops on one foot over the square with the marker in it. (Land with two feet on the double squares.) On the way back, the player picks up the rock and says the name of the book of the Bible in that square.

Step 5: On the second turn, the player throws the marker into the second square, and so forth. The tricky part is staying on one foot when picking up the marker. If a player's foot touches down, then the turn goes to the next player in line. The player leaves her or his marker in the square until the next turn. Also, if the marker doesn't land in the appropriate square, the play goes to the next player in line.

Step 6: The first player to pick up a stone from all the spaces wins the game.

Adapting for more skilled children: With older children, instead of saying the name of the book of the Bible, the player should say the book before and after that book. For example, if "Luke" is in the square, the player would say "Mark and John" as the player retrieves her or his marker.

Bible Book Pop-Up

Instructions

You will need:
  Books of the Bible Cards (pages 56–64)
  Books of the Bible Bookshelves (pages 50–51), or Bible

This game can be played with a large number of children or with only a few. With a smaller group, let the children have more than one card.

Step 1: Shuffle the Books of the Bible Cards.

Step 2: Give each child one or more cards.

Step 3: The children sit in a circle either in chairs or on the floor.

Step 4: Begin to read the books of the Bible in order from the Books of the Bible Bookshelves or the table of contents of a Bible.

Step 5: Whenever the teacher reads a book of the Bible, the child who has that card "pops up" and then immediately sits back down before the teacher goes on to the next book.

Step 6: Children have to pay close attention. Mix the cards up and play again, but this time read faster.

Adapting the game: If you have younger children, one or two cards should be plenty to listen for. Older children may be able to listen for as many as five.

Get on the Shelf

Instructions

You will need:
   Books of the Bible Cards (pages 56–64)
   Chairs

This game is particularly good with a larger number of children (ten or more).

Step 1: Shuffle a set of Books of the Bible Cards. Arrange the chairs in a circle in the center of an open space.

Step 2: Each child selects one card and sits in a chair in the circle.

Step 3: Select one child to be IT. Remove IT's chair from the circle and have IT stand in the center of the circle. The center of the circle is referred to as "the shelf."

Step 4: IT names books of the Bible—as many as six (or more if you have a large group) or as few as two. The children who are holding a card for one of the books called come to the center of the circle or "get on the shelf."

Step 5: When IT calls out "Off the shelf!" then each of the children rushes to get back to a chair in the circle. IT tries to get one of those chairs.

Step 6: The child who is left without a chair becomes the next IT.

Adapting for less skilled children: Limit the selection of books of the Bible to one familiar category (such as Old Testament or New Testament). Allow IT to use the Books of the Bible Bookshelves (pages 50–51) as a reference for calling out books.

Books of the Bible Boogie

Instructions

You will need:
   Books of the Bible Cards (pages 56–64)
   Books of the Bible Bookshelves (pages 50–51)
   CD, CD player

This game will help children become more familiar with the categories of the books of the Bible. If the children are unsure of categories, once they have been given their Books of the Bible Card, allow them time to check the Books of the Bible Bookshelves (pages 50–51) for the correct category—Law, History, Prophets, Poetry and Wisdom, Gospels, and so forth. Choose a CD that is lively to encourage the children to move to the music.

Step 1: Shuffle the Books of the Bible Cards. Place them facedown on the table.

Step 2: The children draw a card from the table. This becomes their Boogie Book.

Step 3: The children sit down around the open space. Begin the CD.

Step 4: Call out a category, such as History. The children who are holding a book of the Bible from that category get up and begin to dance.

Step 5: Continue calling out categories until all the children are dancing.

Step 6: If the children enjoy this activity, collect the cards from this round, let them select a second card, and "boogie away."

Backwards Bible Books

Instructions

You will need:
    Books of the Bible Cards (pages 56–64)
    Books of the Bible Bookshelves (pages 50–51)

This game is good for older children who are familiar with the books of the Bible. Allow less secure children time to use the Books of the Bible Bookshelves (pages 50–51). Thinking in reverse order is not a skill that younger children may be comfortable with yet. However, if the children are willing to give it a try, never stand in their way!

Step 1: Shuffle the Books of the Bible Cards and spread them out on the table.

Step 2: The children come forward one at a time and choose a card from the table, saying the name of the book of the Bible on the card.

Step 3: When the teacher says "go," the children arrange themselves in reverse order of the books' placement in the Bible.

Step 4: Use the Books of the Bible Bookshelves chart or a Bible table of contents to check the accuracy of the arrangement.

Step 5: Just for fun, collect the cards from the children and have them repeat Steps 2 through 4.

Books of the Bible Shuffle

Instructions

You will need:
Books of the Bible Cards (pages 56–64)
Two shoe boxes for each child (See options.)
CD, CD player
Bible, or Books of the Bible Bookshelves (page 50–51)

This is another game where it helps if the children are fairly familiar with the books of the Bible, but it can also be played with a smaller number of cards to make it easier.

Step 1: Give each child one Books of the Bible Card and a pair of shoeboxes. Set the other cards aside.

Step 2: The children put one foot in each shoebox.

Step 3: Start the CD. While the CD is playing, the children shuffle around the room.

Step 4: When the CD stops, the children "shuffle" themselves into the correct order according to the cards they are holding.

Step 5: Use the table of contents in the Bible or the Books of the Bible Bookshelves chart to check the accuracy of the order.

Step 6: Children then "shuffle" the cards (trade with one another so that everyone has a different card), and the game starts again.

Cool Options:

For carpet—Use sheets of wax paper. These slide easily.

For tile floors—Use sheets of cardboard, posterboard, or construction paper.

Show-Up at the OK Corral

Instructions

You will need:
  Books of the Bible Cards (pages 56–64)
  Two hoola hoops
  CD player, CD

This is a good game for creating giggles in addition to reinforcing the division of books of the Bible into Old Testament and New Testament. Make sure you have ample space for the children to move around. This game is fun with a larger number of children (ten or more).

Step 1: Designate two children to be the New Testament and the Old Testament.

Step 2: Give each of those two children a hoola hoop. These are the "corrals."

Step 3: Mix up the Books of the Bible Cards.

Step 4: The remaining children draw a card from the deck.

Step 5: Turn on the CD player. When the music stops, the children see how fast they can get into the appropriate hoola hoop according to whether their card is an Old Testament book or a New Testament book. The children may have to squeeze together to get everyone inside. If there are more children than space in the hoola hoops, put the hoops on the floor and have the children put one part of themselves (a hand or a foot) inside the hoop.

Step 6: Just for fun, collect the cards from the children and repeat Steps 3 through 5.

Cool Option: With a larger group of children, choose only the New Testament or the Old Testament. Have each corral represent a category, such as History or Letters. Use the same procedure.

Amoeba Race

Instructions

You will need:
  Books of the Bible Cards (pages 56–64)
  Masking tape

Here's a chance to learn the books of the Bible at a cellular level. This activity can be done as a competition, but it is just as much fun to play without a winner. Try to select an equal number of Old Testament and New Testament books.

Step 1: Select two children to be the nucleus of two amoebas—one Old Testament and one New Testament. Create two 3-feet-wide masking tape squares on the floor on opposite sides of the room.

Step 2: Shuffle the Books of the Bible Cards you have selected and spread them out on the table.

Step 3: The remaining children come forward one at a time and choose a card from the table, saying the name of the book on the card.

Step 4: When the teacher says "go," the children arrange themselves according to whether they are in the New Testament or the Old Testament. The children with the book cards form a "cell wall" around the appropriate nucleus, forming an amoeba. (The group has to be joined together as closely as possible.)

Step 5: The amoeba proceeds to a designated spot in the room, staying joined together. The first "amoeba" to the spot wins the challenge.

Step 6: Just for fun, collect the cards from the children and let the children choose from a different set of cards. Play the game again, selecting different children to be the nucleus of the cells.

Adapting the game: Here's another opportunity to help the children become more familiar with the categories. Select two categories, such as Law and Gospels. Use duplicate cards if you have a large group and want to have even more fun. There is no reason why there can't be two books of Exodus and two books of Matthew in each amoeba.

Squish

Instructions

You will need:
Books of the Bible Cards (pages 56–64)
Tables
Lots of open space

This game can also be done outdoors if the weather permits. The larger the number of children the more fun it is to "squish" all together.

Step 1: Choose an equal number of cards from the Old and New Testaments.

Step 2: Select two children to be the hiders. They can hide anywhere in the room, but it won't make any difference to the game. Limiting the hiding space to under the tables works well.

Step 3: Shuffle the Books of the Bible Cards and spread them out on the table.

Step 4: The remaining children come forward one at a time and choose a card from the table, saying the name of the book on the card.

Step 5: The two children who are the hiders take their places under two tables. When the teacher says "go," the remaining children "find" their section of the Bible (Old Testament or New Testament) and squish together under the table.

Step 6: Just for fun, collect the cards from the children and have them repeat the game with a new set of cards.

Adapting for more skilled children: If the children are familiar with the various categories of Bible books, change the name of the game to "Category Squish." Select two or more children to represent different categories.

Out of Sorts

Instructions

You will need:
Bible Books Category Markers (page 54)
Books of the Bible Cards (pages 56–64)
Masking tape

This game not only reinforces the different categories of the books of the Bible, it is also a team activity. Team activities allow you to pair not-so-skilled children with those who are more confident.

Step 1: Make a copy of the Bible Books Category Markers (page 54). Cut them apart and tape them on different tables.

Step 2: Divide the class into teams. There should be no more than four children on a team.

Step 3: Shuffle the Books of the Bible Cards. Deal an equal number of cards to each team.

Step 4: When the teacher says "go," the children turn up their cards and place them with the correct category markers.

Step 5: The first team that places all of its cards correctly under the categories wins the game.

Adapting the game: You can adapt this game for the amount of space you have available. If moving-about space is limited, give each team a copy of the page of category markers. Have them place the sheet faceup on the table. Then proceed with the game from Step 3. The children won't have to move as much, but they will still reinforce the skill you are trying to teach.

Scattered Dragon Parts

Instructions

You will need:
Books of the Bible Cards (pages 56–64)
Blindfold for each child
Open space free from hazards

This game can be played with six or more children. The more the merrier. If your children have an aversion to blindfolds, simply let them close their eyes. Make sure you have adult "spotters" to keep the sightless children from going off course.

Step 1: Select enough Books of the Bible Cards to match the number of children you have. Make sure the cards are in sequential order. Then mix them up.

Step 2: The children come forward one at a time and choose a card from the table. They memorize the name of the book of the Bible that is on their card.

Step 3: Blindfold all the children. Place them randomly around the open space. Make sure they are not in order.

Step 4: When the teacher says "go," the child who is the first book of the Bible in the sequence you chose becomes the head of the dragon and moves about, looking for the rest of the dragon. The children stand in place and softly say the name of their book of the Bible.

Step 5: As each dragon part (or book) is added in order, the children hold on to the dragon head and move about the room together. When the entire dragon is put together, the game is over.

Giant Board Game

Instructions

You will need:
  Giant Gameboard Layout (page 49)
  Books of the Bible Cards (pages 56–64)
  Number Cube (page 48)
  Paper, markers, masking tape, scissors, tape or glue
  Bibles

Board games are rarely *bor*-ing. They teach children to take turns and to count. Today's game will also help the children improve their Bible skills. This game can be used with a small or large class since the children can play in teams.

Step 1: Using the Giant Gameboard Layout, create a giant gameboard on the floor of your class space using paper game squares. Secure each square to the floor with loops of masking tape.

Step 2: Photocopy the Number Cube. Cut it out and fold it, taping or gluing the sides in place.

Step 3: Select cards from the Books of the Bible Cards to place on the gameboard as indicated by "Card" on the Giant Gameboard Layout.

Step 4: The children throw the Number Cube to see who goes first.

Step 5: The children take turns throwing the cube and moving that number of spaces on the gameboard.

Step 6: If a player lands on a space that has a Books of the Bible Card, the player must say the name aloud, indicate whether the book is in the New Testament or Old Testament, and find that book in the Bible before he or she can have another turn. (For children who are more skilled, you might want to use a kitchen timer and give them an allotted amount of time.)

Step 7: The game is over when everyone gets to the winners' circle.

Cool Option: Have specific Bible references for the children to look up when they land on "Card" spaces. Key these references to the Bible stories the children are learning in Sunday school.

Number Cube

Cut out the Number Cube along the solid lines. Fold along the dotted lines. Glue or tape together.

Giant Gameboard Layout

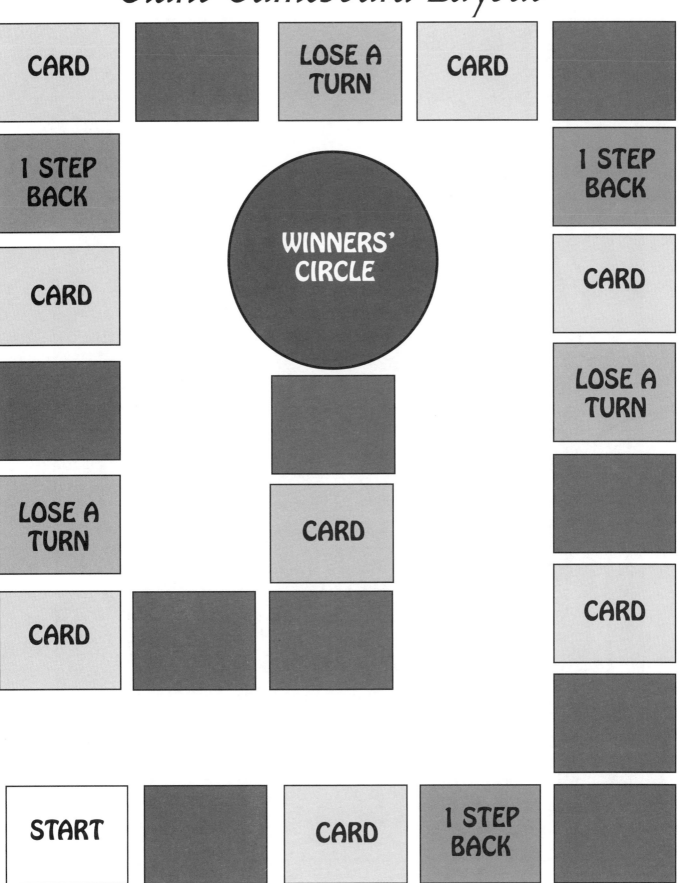

Books of the Bible Bookshelves

Old Testament

Books of Law

GENESIS · EXODUS · LEVITICUS · NUMBERS · DEUTERONOMY

Books of History

JOSHUA · JUDGES · RUTH · 1 SAMUEL · 2 SAMUEL · 1 KINGS · 2 KINGS · 1 CHRONICLES · 2 CHRONICLES · EZRA · NEHEMIAH · ESTHER

Books of Poetry and Wisdom

JOB · PSALMS · PROVERBS · ECCLESIASTES · SONG OF SOLOMON

The Prophets

ISAIAH · JEREMIAH · LAMENTATIONS · EZEKIEL · DANIEL · HOSEA · JOEL · AMOS · OBADIAH · JONAH · MICAH · NAHUM · HABAKKUK · ZEPHANIAH · HAGGAI · ZECHARIAH · MALACHI

Books of the Bible Bookshelves

New Testament

Gospels
MARK
MATTHEW
LUKE
JOHN

History
ACTS OF THE APOSTLES

Letters
ROMANS
1 CORINTHIANS
2 CORINTHIANS
GALATIANS

EPHESIANS
PHILIPPIANS
COLOSSIANS
1 THESSALONIANS
2 THESSALONIANS
1 TIMOTHY
2 TIMOTHY
TITUS
PHILEMON
HEBREWS

JAMES
1 PETER
2 PETER
1 JOHN
2 JOHN
3 JOHN
JUDE

Prophecy
REVELATION

Art: Charles Jakubowski
© 2005 Cokesbury

Scavenger Hunt Questions—Level 1

1. Name one book of the Bible that begins with the letter A.
2. Name the first book of the Old Testament.
3. Name a book of the Bible that has four or fewer letters in its name.
4. Name a book of the Bible that has six or more letters in its name.
5. Name the sixth book of the Old Testament.
6. Name the tenth book of the New Testament.
7. Name a book of the Bible that begins with the letter N.
8. Name a book of the Bible that is named for a woman.
9. Name a book of the Bible that has double letters in its name.
10. Name a book of the Bible that begins with the letter Z.
11. Name a book of the Bible that ends with the letter h.
12. Name a book of the Bible that has two or more s's in its name.
13. Name a book of the Bible that has a 1, 2, or 3 in its name.
14. Name the first book of the New Testament.
15. Name the last book of the Old Testament.
16. Name a book of the Bible that rhymes with *dark*.

Scavenger Hunt Questions—Level 2

1. Name one book of the New Testament of the Bible that is named for a disciple of Jesus.

2. Name the book of the Bible that tells about a man who was swallowed by a big fish.

3. Name the book of the Bible whose name means "beginning."

4. Name the book of the Bible that tells the story of a man who was thrown into a pit of lions.

5. Name a book of the Bible that is a letter from Paul to the church at Corinth, Greece.

6. Name the book of the Bible that is a collection of songs used during worship.

7. Name the book of the Bible that tells about the Hebrew people's escape from slavery in Egypt.

8. Name a book of the Bible that is one of the four Gospels.

9. Name the book of the Bible that would come first if all the books were arranged alphabetically.

10. Name the book of the Bible that would come last if all the books were arranged alphabetically.

11. How many books of the Bible have either a 1, 2, or 3 in front of the name?

12. Name the book of the Bible that is a letter from Paul to the church in Rome, Italy.

13. Name the book of the Bible that tells how Moses' successor led the Hebrew people into the Promised Land.

14. Name a book of the Bible where you would find some of the first kings of Israel.

15. Name a book of the Bible where you would expect to find stories about Jesus, what he taught, what he did, and who he knew.

16. Name a book of the Bible where you would expect to find stories about the first apostles and what they did after Jesus went to be with God.

Bible Books Category Markers

Law	Gospels
O.T. History	N.T. History
Poetry and Wisdom	Letters
O.T. Prophecy	N.T. Prophecy

Books of the Bible Cards

Books of the
Old Testament

Genesis

Exodus

Leviticus

Numbers

Deuteronomy

Joshua

Judges

Ruth	1 Samuel
2 Samuel	1 Kings
2 Kings	1 Chronicles
2 Chronicles	Ezra

Nehemiah	Esther
Job	Psalms
Proverbs	Ecclesiastes
Song of Solomon	Isaiah

Jeremiah	Lamentations
Ezekiel	Daniel
Hosea	Joel
Amos	Obadiah

Jonah	Micah
Nahum	Habakkuk
Zephaniah	Haggai
Zechariah	Malachi

Books of the New Testament 👇	Matthew
Mark	Luke
John	Acts of the Apostles
Romans	1 Corinthians

2 Corinthians	Galatians
Ephesians	Philippians
Colossians	1 Thessalonians
2 Thessalonians	1 Timothy

2 Timothy	Titus
Philemon	Hebrews
James	1 Peter
2 Peter	1 John

2 John	3 John
Jude	Revelation